D0576727

POLAND

A PICTURE MEMORY

Text
Tim Sharman

Design
Teddy Hartshorn

Photography
Colour Library Books Ltd
FPG International
International Stock Photo
Tim Sharman
Woodfin Camp and Associates, Inc

Picture Editor
Annette Lerner

Commissioning Editor
Andrew Preston

Editorial
Fleur Robertson
Louise Houghton

Production
Ruth Arthur
David Proffit
Sally Connolly

Director of Production
Gerald Hughes

Director of Publishing
David Gibbon

CLB 2576
© 1990 Colour Library Books Ltd, Godalming, Surrey, England.
All rights reserved.
Color separations by Scantrans Pte Ltd, Singapore.
This 1990 edition published by Crescent Books,
distributed by Outlet Book Company, Inc, a Random House Company,
225 Park Avenue South, New York, New York 10003.
ISBN 0 517
87654321

POLAND
A PICTURE MEMORY

CRESCENT BOOKS
NEW YORK

First page and previous pages: the foothills of the Tatra mountains. Facing page: the garden of Chopin's birthplace, in Żelazowa Wola.

A visitor to Poland's green and rolling countryside, with its tiny, hand-carved fields, its villages stranded in sandy forests and its army of hard-working horses, could be forgiven for thinking that this is a land that history has passed by. The truth, however, is otherwise. Almost every storm of Europe's turbulent past has touched this country, forging a nation of tough survivors and fierce patriots aware of their own identity and rich cultural heritage.

Krzysztof Daniel is a typically proud young Pole. Several times each week he climbs two-hundred feet up rickety stairs in one of the country's most famous churches, and, from a gallery overlooking the medieval heart of Kraków, Poland's former capital, he marks the hours with trumpet calls to the four quarters. Each time, at exactly the same place, the call is cut short. Legend has it that it was at that point, in the year 1241, that an arrow from the approaching Mongol army pierced the throat of the city guard as he sounded the alarm.

This ritual, broadcast nationally at noon each day, reveals several aspects of Polish history and character. The ever-present fear of attack from the east and the west; the long memory of events that is never allowed to fade; the love and respect – even the need – for heroes and martyrs – all this can be read into that clarion call from Poland's most fascinating city. Kraków escaped damage in the Second World War; its rich interiors, wonderful Flemish tapestries and countless mansions and churches survive intact to make it one of the loveliest cities in the land.

Warsaw, Poland's capital city since the early seventeenth century, was not so fortunate. In the summer of 1944, as the Soviets gathered to take the city, the long-suffering citizens rose up against their Nazi occupiers. After two months of bitter fighting, involving both young and old alike, the rising was crushed and the whole of the Old Town area, and much else besides, was deliberately burned and blasted to rubble by the Germans. Nearly 200,000 people died. Now, though, only old photographs in museums reveal those terrible days because, in yet another heroic gesture of defiance, the Poles rebuilt their capital brick by brick, copying exactly what had been there before. Using old drawings and photographs and even the eighteenth-century paintings of Bernardo Bellotto, nephew to the great Canaletto, whose detailed paintings of Warsaw were hidden during the war, they miraculously pieced together their lovely city.

Today the narrow streets, the tall churches and the great, pink-painted Royal Palace stand proudly again on the high west bank of the Vistula. Throughout the country this pattern of reconstruction continued. Gdansk, the handsome port at the mouth of the Vistula, the place where the first shots of World War Two were fired, also re-emerged from utter devastation. Sadly, the immense effort and expertise involved at the time was not matched by sensible investment in industry. Today the economy is handicapped by the need to support numerous outmoded heavy industries which were built according to Stalinist philosophies.

The past two hundred years have not been happy ones for a country which was once the largest in Europe. Those glorious centuries, when Kraków was one of the brightest courts and liveliest seats of learning on the continent, faded. In 1683 King Jan Sobieski was an international hero for saving Vienna, and consequently Central Europe, from the clutches of the Turkish Army. Yet by 1795 the country was a political shambles and Poland's mighty and ambitious neighbors, Prussia, Russia and Austria, had partitioned the kingdom and the name of Poland was removed from the map. There followed 120 years of foreign rule, during which the Poles served three masters and only the Austrian-controlled regions allowed the Polish language to be taught in schools. As so often happens, adversity strengthened and unified the country; the Polish nation in the nineteenth century produced many artists and writers of international stature – all, in one way or another, inspired by the country's political repression. Most prominent among these were the poets Adam Mickiewicz, Juliusz Slowacki and Cyprian Norwid, the painter Jan Matejko and the universally loved composer Fryderyk Chopin.

Emerging from the chaos of the First World War damaged but unbowed, there were only twenty years of uncertain peace for Poland under the autocratic leadership of the extraordinary and romantic patriot Józef Pilsudski before it all happened again. Hitler's *Blitzkrieg* brushed aside the Polish army from the west and Stalin rolled in from the east. Once again Poland was a battlefield. Six million Poles – eighteen percent of the population – died in the Second World War. The names Auschwitz and Majdanek, Sobibór and Treblinka

– all death camps erected by the Nazis on Polish soil – are etched into the very soul of the nation. Poles visiting the West are shocked that children do not know of these events, for neither they nor their children's children will ever be allowed to forget them. Yet despite the awfulness of their experiences, the Polish spirit survived the Nazi horrors as it had the years of partition.

Perhaps the greatest miracle of Polish history is that so much of value has survived the devastations so often visited upon the country. From the amber-bearing beaches of the Baltic Sea down to the rocky barrier of the Carpathians; from the Odra River in the west to the great forests and marshes which border the Soviet Union, Poland is studded with marvelous palaces and castles, churches, monasteries and market towns. Warsaw and Kraków, Gdansk and Poznan are great European cities with fine universities, museums and art collections, wonderful Gothic cathedrals and elegant Renaissance town halls. From the wooden churches of the south to remote Frombork far away on the Baltic coast where Copernicus re-invented the universe, there are countless exquisite places with unique architecture and an atmosphere unlike anything in western Europe.

And in between these towns, far out on dusty roads, up steep mountain tracks or beside winding narrow gauge railways, there are the villages of Poland. The collectivized agriculture so beloved of socialist planners was long ago rejected by the stubborn Polish farmers, poor as they were, and to this day most land is cultivated by families wedded to the soil. Here the old ways survive. Traditional costume is often worn to church and market, even by young people. In the Tatra mountains, for example, a precarious living is eked out of thin soil 3,000 feet above sea level, but a wedding here will reveal a rich culture, reflected in lively music and dance and colorfully embroidered clothes fashioned during the long, snowbound winters.

In Poland's cities young people may wear jeans and listen to jazz and rock music, but there is still a formality and gentility to life and family bonds are strong. Flowers are always taken when visiting, hands are kissed and men often embrace upon meeting. Old rules of hospitality also survive, and a meal with a family can be a lesson in manners. Christmas and Easter are the social and religious highlights for this devout and mainly Catholic society. Then, a complex round of visiting is matched by skill and hard work in the kitchen as innumerable dishes are prepared for the days of celebration. At Easter beautifully decorated eggs are taken to crowded church ceremonies to be blessed.

This great strength of tradition, which survives present day city life in often cramped apartment blocks, quite obviously draws upon a long and well-recorded history. A glance at the map will help to explain much of Poland's troubled past. For thousands of years on the great plain of Northern Europe various tribes have pushed and shoved in an effort to make a more secure home for themselves. Situated between the often-changing German federations and the later-developing Russia, the fortunes of the Poles have ebbed and flowed in relation to the power and ambitions of their neighbors.

The emergence of the Poles as a recognisable nation state dates from the tenth century when their leader, King Mieszko I, married a Bohemian princess and, as part of the deal, accepted Christianity. From then on, the nation's history is well documented and much is known about the various kings and princes, both good, bad and merely incompetent, who have ruled the land. Despite many frontier changes over the centuries, the last of which was in 1945 when the whole country shifted westward, Poland today occupies almost exactly the same tract of land as it did a thousand years ago. The fifteenth century saw Polish control at its greatest extent, stretching from the Baltic to the Black Sea, and during the following two centuries the kingdom was a mighty power in the region.

The very first power base of the early kings, and the region often referred to as the cradle of the Polish state, lay in what is now the west of the country around the city of Poznan. Archaeological finds here have revealed many traces of the highly organized Lusatian culture which flourished some 2,500 years ago, and at Biskupin a settlement from that period has been reconstructed on the original timber foundations which were preserved in the mud of a lake. The nearby town of Gniezno was Mieszko's first capital and the place where, in 966, his conversion took place. Although small, it is still the seat of the Polish primate. Much legend surrounds Miezko's ancestors, the strangest telling of the evil Popiel who was eaten by mice when locked in a dungeon by his brother Piast. The latter gave his name to the dynasty which ruled Poland until 1385.

The conversion to Roman Catholicism brought the fledgling Poland firmly within the sphere of Western culture. Although artistic influences from the Greek Orthodox world were felt via the neighboring Russian principalities, and there was even contact with Islam through trade with the Turkish-controlled regions of southeast Europe, Poland has always looked westward for artistic, as well as political, inspiration. Throughout the country the traveler will come across examples of all styles of European architecture and decoration, from the Romanesque through Gothic, Renaissance and Baroque to the Neo-classical of the nineteenth century. The great cathedral at Gniezno, for example, boasts a pair of decorated bronze doors from the twelfth century which are amongst the finest and most important examples of Romanesque metalwork in Europe, while Gdansk has one of the continent's largest Gothic churches. Countless smaller churches, monasteries and town halls contain exquisite craftsmanship, reflecting the growing power and importance of the Polish state in the later Middle Ages.

Having suffered several invasions from Bohemia, however, the capital was moved to the relative security of Kraków in 1038. This long-established market town, built on a trade route which stretched eastward to Persia, became the focus of Polish development for the next five hundred years. So rich is the city in artistic and historical treasures that an eighteenth-century visitor did not exaggerate when he wrote "Even had no history of Polish lands ever been written, it could largely be read in its walls and stones." Fourteen Polish kings were buried in the cathedral on Wawel Hill, their tombs and chapels all masterpieces of sculpture.

The castle next door, rebuilt in the first years of the sixteenth century, is a happy amalgam of Italian and Polish styles and was home to the golden age of Polish civilization, attracting artists, musicians and scholars from many countries. Today Wawel is a magnificent museum and a magnet for visitors from around the world, as is the nearby Old Town of Kraków, with its vast market square, magnificent Renaissance cloth hall and, of course, the Mariacki church whence our trumpeter sounds his plaintive alarm.

In that pre-industrial age, Poland's wealth lay in the export of grain to Western Europe by way of the Baltic. At the heart of this business, as it has been at the heart of the nation since its beginnings, is the Vistula, which rises in the Carpathian Mountains and rolls northwards for 500 miles before meeting the sea at Gdansk. To journey down this strong, brown river is to trace both the geography and history of the country and provide a panorama of life in Poland today.

From the wild, forested hills which mark the frontier with Czechoslovakia the young river drops quickly to an undulating plain, passing close to Oswiecim, which the Germans called Auschwitz, and the little town of Wadowice where Pope John Paul II was born in the spring of 1920. At Kraków the broadening stream flows beneath the castle and cathedral and then follows a great arc through the soft and lush pastures of eastern Poland. The river here borders family farms, each based upon just a few acres of rich black soil; an agricultural landscape interrupted by the occasional small town, such as Sandomierz and Kazimierz, which for centuries guarded the crossing points of ancient trade routes. This was the Polish corn belt and the region is still thick with great houses built by landowning nobles and filled with fine furniture, tapestries and paintings from Italy, Germany and the Netherlands. The great soldier and statesman Jan Zamoyski went so far as to build for himself an ideal city which would reflect his wealth and power and become a center for trade and learning. Built by Italian architects, Zamosc today is one of the best-preserved Renaissance towns in Europe, its large square lined with pastel painted houses and its skyline pierced by spires.

Beyond Warsaw, the river passes more ancient monasteries and picturesque towns, including medieval Torun, the birthplace of Copernicus. Then, before entering the sea, it slides beneath the great red-brick bulk of Malbork, the largest Gothic fortress in Europe, built in the thirteenth century as a headquarters for the invading Teutonic Knights, a powerful group of militant Christians who tormented Poland for several centuries.

In most countries of Europe extensive church building is a thing of the past, but in devout Poland the recent years have witnessed a quite incredible program which has bequeathed to the landscape a few elegant, modernistic structures, but also a large number of costly and extremely unpleasant concrete churches, many inappropriately placed in small villages. Yet so large is this country that such aberrations are easily absorbed. Generally speaking, Poles care deeply about their countryside and for many years there have been national parks, thirteen in all, giving special protection to particularly beautiful and valuable regions.

The most dramatic of these parks embraces the alpine peaks of the Tatra Mountains, with their glacial lakes, golden eagles and occasional brown bear. A favorite holiday center for both climbers and skiers, the foothills around the resort town of Zakopane, speckled with unique wooden villages and churches, are especially beautiful. Several other wilderness areas of the Carpathian Range, which marks the country's southern border, are protected zones, enabling the flora and fauna, which includes marmot, lynx and eagle owls, to live undisturbed.

One of Poland's greatest attractions is the extensive network of shallow lakes which spans the entire north of the country. There are thousands of them, many linked by natural waterways, and in summer they are a paradise for sailors and canoeists. In winter hardy souls go ice-sailing here in temperatures which drop far below zero. Formed by the retreating ice sheets of the last ice age and spreading across the border into Lithuania, the Mazurian lakes merge into the last remaining tract of primeval woodland in Europe. The unique landscape of the Bialowieza Forest, home to the beaver and bison, the tarpan and elk, is a reservoir of wildlife and owes its survival to the old nobles who preserved it for hunting.

There are two parks amongst the often wild dunes of the Baltic coast which provide a crucial habitat for such rare creatures as the sea eagle, while Warsaw has on its doorstep a vast stretch of protected pine forest, bordered by the Vistula, which was often used as a sanctuary in times of war.

Yet all is not sweetness and light along the Vistula, for as well as representing the continuity of the Polish state it is also a symbol of the ills which beset the country today. Forty-five years of bad industrial design and management has left Poland a victim of that scourge of the age, industrial pollution. Kraków, having survived the centuries intact, is most at risk. The factories and coalfields of nearby Silesia combine with a local grossly inefficient steelworks to pour acid rain on the city, stripping the cathedral roof of its gold, dissolving the very stones of its churches, mansions and statues and, of course, poisoning its people.

Fortunately, all this is no longer an official secret and, under the new Solidarity-based regime, plans are in hand that will restore the city to its rightful place as one of Europe's showpieces, while generally improving the standard of life throughout the country. Despite the enormity of both their economic and political problems, do not doubt that the indefatigable Poles will overcome them and once again stand proud as a great and independent power in the new Europe which is now taking shape.

Facing page: A Baltic Coast resort.

Most of Poland's 250-mile Baltic Coast (these pages and overleaf) consists of inhospitable sand dunes, but since time immemorial it has been a rich source of the golden fossilized resin, amber.

Gdańsk (these pages), the only city on the Baltic Coast, is best known today for its shipyard (right), the birthplace of the Solidarity movement, but it has been a port and trading center for a thousand years. Gdańsk's Golden Age was in the sixteenth century, when it was one of Europe's richest cities. The many splendid burghers' houses were built at this time, and the town hall (facing page) achieved its imposing grandeur. The first shots of World War II were fired here, and by 1945 much of the town had been destroyed, but has been rebuilt since in all of its old glory.

Facing page: Gdańsk's fourteenth-century Gothic St. Catherine's Church and Great Mill.

Below: the 1444 crane on Gdańsk's waterfront. Overleaf: the Baltic lagoon at Frombork.

17

Frombork (facing page), on the eastern Baltic Coast, is dominated by the fourteenth-century Gothic cathedral (facing page bottom), where Copernicus was once deacon. For centuries the northern region was a battlefield – hence the Gothic fortifications at Olsztyn (right and above right). The years of Prussian occupation have also influenced architecture (below) in Olsztyn. Napoleon stayed at the little town of Pułtusk (below right) on his fateful Russian expedition of 1812. Above: picturesque Szczytno. Overleaf: thirteenth-century Malbork Castle, the largest Gothic fortress in Europe and once the headquarters of the Teutonic Knights.

In much of the Polish countryside, traditional values and lifestyles survive, and nowhere more so than in the southern mountains. The richly decorated costumes seen at a wedding (facing page, above, above right and right) in the village of Bukowina are still commonplace for such special events. The fine needlework is done during the long, snowbound winter months. Accompanied by much music and vodka, such ceremonies may last many days. The cities also know how to celebrate, the most spectacular occasion being the June festival (below and below right) in the southern city of Kraków.

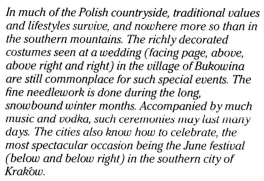

The great Northern Plain of Europe, shaped by the last ice age and traversed by a chain of several thousand lakes, stretches across Poland from the German to the Soviet border. Much of the region is forested, and on small private farms (left) the thin, sandy soil is still worked using horses rather than motor vehicles. Typical of these often remote villages is Kruszyniany (center left), where this old barn is being re-thatched. In the east, the lake district of Mazuria (bottom left and below) is popular with holidaymakers and sailors alike, the network of waterways providing endless scope for wilderness sailing.

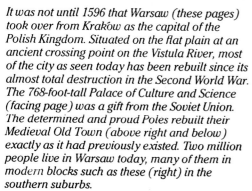

It was not until 1596 that Warsaw (these pages) took over from Kraków as the capital of the Polish Kingdom. Situated on the flat plain at an ancient crossing point on the Vistula River, most of the city as seen today has been rebuilt since its almost total destruction in the Second World War. The 768-foot-tall Palace of Culture and Science (facing page) was a gift from the Soviet Union. The determined and proud Poles rebuilt their Medieval Old Town (above right and below) exactly as it had previously existed. Two million people live in Warsaw today, many of them in modern blocks such as these (right) in the southern suburbs.

Warsaw's heyday was during the eighteenth century, before its lasting partition by Prussia, Russia and Austria removed it from the map until 1918. An elegant city of boulevards, palaces and parks, Warsaw was much visited by Europe's aristocracy, and was home to many artists and writers. Royal summer palaces were built in Łazienki Park (facing page bottom) and at Wilanów (facing page top, above and below). Top left: the city symbol; (left) the Jewish Ghetto Memorial and (below left) the Chopin Statue, beside which recitals of the great man's music are given. Overleaf: the restored market place of the Old Town.

Below: Syrenka, Warsaw's symbol: a mythological mermaid supposed to have founded the city.

The Vistula River (facing page top) runs through Warsaw before reaching the Mazowsze Plain (facing page bottom).

Poland is a devoutly religious nation – the majority of its people being of the Roman Catholic faith. Countless church festivals, such as those in the small towns of Łowicz (left) and Kadzidło (above left, above and below left), bring out the older generation, attired in their traditional finery. The election of a Polish Pope in 1978 strengthened the role of the church in society. The country's most revered icon is the Byzantine portrait, known as the Black Madonna (below), at the Jasna Góra monastery in southern Poland. In the east, centuries of Russian influence have resulted in there being many followers of the Eastern Orthodox Church (facing page).

Many towns in the southeast of Poland were developed on ancient trade routes connecting Russia with Central Europe. Chief of these is Lublin, a twelfth-century fortress, whose town centre (above, above right and below) is one of the most atmospheric in Poland. The original castle (facing page top), was rebuilt in the nineteenth century in a neo-Gothic style. Charming Kazimierz Dolny (right) nestles beside the Vistula River, whereas Zamość (below right) is a splendid example of Renaissance town planning. Facing page bottom: Ojców, a village in the low, limestone hills of southern Poland.

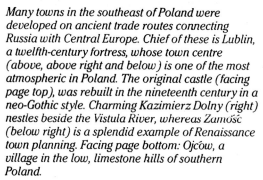

The lands around the southern city of Kraków are known as "little Poland" and were one of the places where the Polish State was founded a thousand years ago. The soft landscape of woods and fields is dotted with small farms, mercifully saved from collectivisation during Communist rule. Life is governed by the seasons here, and family and friends all turn out to help with the harvest, which is often gathered by hand. Farmers collect water in horse-drawn tankers (left) in the remote village of Pilica (remaining pictures).

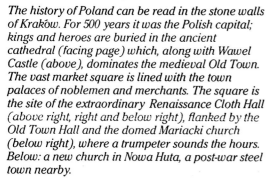

The history of Poland can be read in the stone walls of Kraków. For 500 years it was the Polish capital; kings and heroes are buried in the ancient cathedral (facing page) which, along with Wawel Castle (above), dominates the medieval Old Town. The vast market square is lined with the town palaces of noblemen and merchants. The square is the site of the extraordinary Renaissance Cloth Hall (above right, right and below right), flanked by the Old Town Hall and the domed Mariacki church (below right), where a trumpeter sounds the hours. Below: a new church in Nowa Huta, a post-war steel town nearby.

The industrial suburbs have changed Kraków (these pages) into a large and busy city. In its medieval heart (above left), however, the modern world is kept at bay and flower sellers do a good trade – the Poles taking flowers whenever they go visiting. Left: villagers still bring their produce to the city's markets. During the nineteenth century, partitioned Kraków – under Austrian rule – was home to writers and artists struggling to free their nation. Today the fight is against polution, which attacks the city from both the local Nowa Huta steelworks and the great industrial region of Silesia to the west.

Country life in Poland is simple (these pages), but many farmers are relatively prosperous. It is possible to travel all day without seeing a motor vehicle – although hard-working horses abound. Bred privately and traded at the many country markets, a horse is a major family investment and is well looked after. Most families also keep a cow, which they tether by the quiet verges to graze all day and then walk home in the evening (bottom left). It is likely that the young children outside the village shop (center left) will leave home to find higher education and a career.

Toruń (facing page), on the Vistula River in north Poland, is an historical town with a rich architectural heritage. Dating back to the thirteenth century, Toruń was founded by the Teutonic Knights. Copernicus, the great astronomer, was born to a merchant family of this town in 1473, and its university bears his name today. Rural life has its own rewards (this page), whether it be a glass of wine (right) after a long day, or the tranquility of the view in the Holy Cross Mountains (below right). Overleaf: Niedzica Castle, once the guardian of Poland's mountainous southern frontier.

52

Poland's southern boundary with Czechoslovakia follows the watershed of the Carpathian Mountains, which reach alpine proportions in the Tatra Range (these pages), where peaks top 8,000 feet. Nowadays popular with hikers, climbers and skiers, the rugged slopes and their wooded foothills were a refuge for partisans in the Second World War. The final shots of that war were fired in 1947 by Ukrainian patriots in the desolate Bieszczady Hills of southeast Poland. The beautiful Podhale region beneath the High Tatra is full of charming rural villages, some of which (overleaf) are becoming more popular as tourist spots.

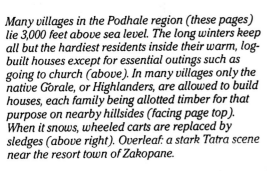

Many villages in the Podhale region (these pages) lie 3,000 feet above sea level. The long winters keep all but the hardiest residents inside their warm, log-built houses except for essential outings such as going to church (above). In many villages only the native Górale, or Highlanders, are allowed to build houses, each family being allotted timber for that purpose on nearby hillsides (facing page top). When it snows, wheeled carts are replaced by sledges (above right). Overleaf: a stark Tatra scene near the resort town of Zakopane.

The highland people consider themselves almost a race apart, with their own distinctive culture (these pages). There is little money to be made from farming the thin soil, but additional income can be earned from folk crafts such as embroidery, wood carving and glass painting. The exciting music produced here is played mainly at the villagers' own ceremonies, though a popular folk festival is held in Zakopane (below left). Facing page bottom: in spring the mountain valleys are thick with wild flowers. The busiest time comes in autumn, when everyone lends a hand to harvest the hay and the potato crop (overleaf and final page).